HOW TO BE FREE
FROM CONCERN
By Nick Withycombe

Disclaimer
None of the contents of this or any other material
by the author is intended as medical advice.
Always seek professional guidance on matters of
health.

Table of Contents

Nick Withycombe

So You Want To Be Free From Concern...

This is about **awareness.**

You've seen the title of the book and wanted to know more. It means that you've already started a journey of well-being: you have awareness of your own state of mind.

To already have recognised that you experience anxiety, stress and pressure – and that you want to be free from concern – is a decent place to be. It also means that I'm going to make an assumption: that you're of sufficiently sound mind and logical capacity to realise that we may, most likely, never be completely free from concern.

We're worriers. For whatever genetic or formative reason, our minds are quick to fret. Paranoia is part of life. Anxiety doesn't have to be a special guest in our lives, but it hums in the background and can be a baseline to our thoughts, no matter how well we are, on the whole.

This also means that this book is not a case of the writer – that's me – guiding you up the mountain of mental imbalance up to the peak of eternal happiness and delight. Of course, I am not 100% free from concern. But, through experience and relentless internal conversation, I have at least pitched my well-being tent onto the plateau of solid all-round health. Nice, right.

How To Be Free From Concern

So to keep the metaphor going just because I feel like it, I am happy to be your Sherpa of solace, sharing what I've learned about coping with a head full of complete nonsense, about being in a world that doesn't make sense and about having a goal to live, as much as possible, free from concern.

Nick Withycombe

UNDERSTANDING WHAT BEING FREE FROM CONCERN MEANS

This is absolutely not about 'not giving a f*ck' but about how you can have better mental well-being and therefore live a fuller, better life.

Being free from concern does not mean rejecting all society or throwing your hands up in the air and letting your responsibilities or care for others drop to the ground.

It's not about a definition of what makes a good or bad person – such as good people suffer anxiety because they care, but egotistical people are bad. I'm working on another assumption that if you're reading this you are suffering in some sense – whether mildly or worse – from a continual, general weight of concern and you would like to think about how you can live without it.

Generally speaking, I've found that people who are 'bad' lack any concern and live in their own head, while 'good' people, unfortunately, are the ones who are suffering mentally, often due to over-thinking situations, or from caring a lot. It's one reason why the world is the way it is; people who are power-hungry and self-serving can rise to the top (e.g. of politics), while people who just like to be nice to others are content with the life they have.

But this isn't about that particular problem. Our

goal here is to stay responsible and still 'be concerned' for the good of others and the Earth as a whole – but to be free from negativity, doubt, paranoia, a lack of confidence and concern in our own minds.

It should also be said that if the concern you experience is

debilitating or incapacitating then you should seek professional medical help – that's what they're there for.

SKIPPING OVER THE SCIENCE

The amygdala is the part of the brain that induces the fight or flight response, blocking the frontal lobes from making reasoned, thoughtful decisions and telling your adrenal glands to produce adrenaline and cortisol. So, when we are nervous or fearful, we make less intelligent decisions.

I've never found this information to be helpful. I know that my concern is there because I am human, and we've evolved quickly so that we are still animals yet we can sit and ponder the meaning of life. Sentient meat. This contradiction and the existentialism that it produces doesn't free me from concern. What it can do, for society and the individual too (you), is normalise concern.

Normalising concern doesn't help us to be free from it – but it helps the most extreme situations or cases. No one should think 'I am so worried and I must make it stop' or 'my anxiety means something is wrong with me', but instead realise that it's normal to be concerned. It's something to put under the microscope, talk about out loud and think about in the context of your nature versus nurture make-up.

AND WHY?

Being free from concern seems like an obvious benefit in life, but being free from concern does not mean receding from life. This book is not a survival guide or 90 pages on how to be a hoarder for when society may crumble. You can still thrive on challenge, take

risks and try new things without the dangerous belief that going out of your comfort zone must be 'where the magic happens' – I enjoy a rant on that one later on.

The belief is that being free from concern allows you to be successful in life – I refer to success quite a bit; with this, of course, being your definition of what success means to you on a daily and whole-life basis. This book is not like certain social media accounts that fetishise failure or dramaticise 'adulting', celebrating the notion that 'life is hard' and aren't we all a little bit pathetic really so that's OK? The goal is to be fully self-aware, to live life without nagging doubts, without simmering paranoia and uneven levels of confidence.

The optimistic idea is that you, I, we, can be aware of our pursuit to be free from concern.

The Musings –
Trying To Make Sense
Of The Mental Ascent

Nick Withycombe

Being Free of Concern From Yourself

This is about **acceptance.**

Much of being free from concern relates to how you can interact with the rest of humanity. But first thing's first – you need to free yourself from the concerns that blossom in your own brain. These happen thanks to nature, nurture and the odd situation that we find ourselves in: being basically animalistic but with the ability (and tendency) to contemplate the meaning of life.

Of all the funny parts of our psyche, I am personally not a fan of the ego. If our goal is to be free from concern, to find our success and make the world a better place, I believe that there is promise to be found in removing it from our psychological structure. Or, if not entirely removing then at least being aware of it – and not paying it much attention.

Removing your ego can be a good thing to do for these assumptions:

- More evolved societies are based on their superego (morality) and lesser ones – let's say during medieval times
  – are based on their id and their ego (their base drives and how they feel they can get them).
- It is good to be a more evolved, developed and civilised person
- Ego is a childish weakness and I am an adult
- Being egocentric makes the world a worse

place

- You can find calm, peace and satisfaction by moving to your superego
- Even if you want to please your id then it is better to do this via your superego

Essentially, this theory is saying:

YOUR ID

Of course you have an id, as you are a creature and therefore have basic drives to eat, sleep, procreate and pleasure your senses through comfort and experiences that your brain enjoys. These basic drives are not bad, and they do not have to be totally animal. Recognising that you have them does not necessarily mean that you are going to act on them. Of course, some people do – but the fact that they are 'basic' simply means that they are foundations of your existential construct. You can still manage how you achieve and obtain them.

As explained in the excellent Wikipedia definition: "The id (Latin for "it", German: Es) is the disorganised part of the personality structure that contains a human's basic, instinctual drives. Id is the only component of personality that is present from birth."

The id was recognised as the source of our simplest impulses and desires, such as sexual and aggressive drives.

YOUR EGO

Your ego looks at how you can get these basic drives, as well as how you feel about yourself and the world around you. Quoting Freud, the Wikipedia page explains how the ego has defense mechanisms to use when society's current morals, norms and taboos stop them from getting what their id is driving them towards. It lists these as "denial, displacement, intellectualisation, fantasy, compensation, projection, rationalization, reaction formation, regression, repression, and sublimation".

There are even more of these not-very-positive sounding characteristics, but basically put, the ego leads to the following traits: easily taking offence, believing oneself to be high and mighty, thinking of oneself as superior, unable to listen to other people's opinions and so on. Essentially, taking yourself too seriously and thinking about yourself a lot.

This then overflows into outright narcissism. Not to be confused with vanity, which isn't the worst thing in the world (and could be something that shy, nervous or concerned people might exercise to boost their self-image), narcissism is the love of oneself to the specific detriment of others.

SUPEREGO

The superego was traditionally explained in

How To Be Free From Concern

Freudian terms from the side of self-control in a negative sense – as if the superego only causes guilt or 'punishment' if we feel we are doing something wrong. But it doesn't have to only be about that.

The superego has been accused of aiming for perfection from the perspective of it wanting to achieve an ideal state. But the aim of perfection is not the same thing as the demand for it. You can try to do something the very best you can – perfection being your effort – with full realisation that you may not achieve it – and you can feel OK about that.

The superego criticises the ego. It is the conscience of evolved people. Freud accused the superego of prohibiting drives, fantasies, feelings and actions, because at that time in the world (1850 or so), the id (base drives and wants) and ego (belief about getting them) were believed to be naughty, and we, the plebian population, were little more than cattle. Today, there are some people on the planet who have 'good' base drives and wants, and the concept of sex has evolved to be something other than the filthy, dirty, silent deed it was back in the prudish, priggish and puritanical days of yore.

While it was an amazing break-through in the understanding of the human psyche by Freud, the id-ego-superego original theory was conceived, by definition, at the time of Freud. This means that the description of the superego has too much of a focus on its control of our "forbidden" urges – only because most urges were forbidden in the prissy, prim and niminy-piminy 1800s. Today, I prefer to look at the superego from the positive side; i.e. letting us analyse our own thoughts based on the a more evolved perspective of morality and civilisation.

HOW DO THESE WORK IN MODERN LIFE?

Once we have an understanding of the structure of our mind, we can think about how we are going to best make use of our superego in daily life.

IN LIFE

Success can be found by self-awareness (which includes self- knowledge); understanding what you want and why – and then looking into how you can realistically achieve this. We'll go into this later.
Breaking down your own psychology – of what you want and why you want it – comes with an understanding of your own personal id, and your superego analysing the rights and wrongs of this, in terms of how it impacts those around you.

Without this 'id to superego' relationship, your ego might reduce you to childish or un-intellectual actions. Not that being childish means all childlike traits are bad, but we're assuming that adults should progress beyond the urges and non-consequential thinking of a child.

This is not only looking the theory of 'how you will achieve the success that you want', it's about how you act every day, in your interactions with other people and 'the world' – which includes what you consume from the news, in media, around you.
Using your superego means calmly analysing each interaction, each situation, looking at why people

are acting as they are acting, and how you may best respond to find success. This is in contrast to the ego, which would cause you to only think of how you can quickly 'get what you want' out of the situation, or 'what this means for me' at any given moment, or essentially uncontrolled reactions and urges that you do not put any thought into, instead purely basing them on either 'I liked that' or 'I did not like that'.

Doing this can ease your concern because you are able to remove yourself from simply having immediate reactions to situations. This ability to take a moment (or longer) for consideration lets you plan your reaction – or possibly inaction – which can lead to a less anxiety-causing consequence.

AT WORK

Removing your ego in a work situation can be a great thing to do
– it's essentially taking the high road of any situation, looking long-term and removing your more childish emotions from the situation.

Everyone knows those people who, in life and therefore at work, are self-centred, looking to achieve a promotion (more power and money) however they can, even if it means doing so in uncivilised ways. One assumption might be that people who are incredibly self-centred are free from concern, because they don't seem to be bothered by hurting others or how their reputation develops in the long-term. Yet, I've often observed that these people simply live with another kind of ego-based concern that they need the world to see them as clever and powerful.

Meanwhile, human nature ensures that some people (or most/all in certain societies) in the 'boss' position are prone to allowing their ego to control their actions, thoughts and take centre stage, because so many of their ego-based actions can result in a positive reinforcement that pleases their id. This can be simply represented by 'manager jokes'.

So very many times in my life have I seen people in the boss position make un-funny jokes that cause the staff to laugh with energetic gusto, and so they believe they are funny. I have lived/worked in societies where this is especially distinct, where the underlings will do pretty much anything to please the ego of their boss. I have seen people try to appear what is seen as 'good' by society, yet in reality be completely the opposite behind closed doors. This isn't blaming them for doing so, it's just the way it is, and the way for them to achieve more money to use in life.

Being in a position of power can lead a person to feed their ego, without any higher figure or some form of boundary reminding them that their ego is growing out of control.

In the workplace environment, removing your ego does contain risks. You can see it in the same way as fear – as intelligent people, we understand that fear itself is a weakness and can stop us from achieving. Yet on the other hand, fear can be wise, because it keeps us safe.

Your ego can perform a similar function – the weaknesses it presents can hold you back in terms of evolution and development and happiness, yet, it can be a protective tool or defensive weapon when faced by the ego of others. This is where the 'setting out your stall' or the 'f*** you position' comes into play, which we'll talk about later.

While the boss can enjoy having their ego fed by the idea that they are always right, this simply breeds resentment as the staff see that their leader thinks 'I pay, I say', and just because essentially one is in control of the other's livelihood, their word is final.

So, although I've advocated for the removal of ego above, the workplace setting is one where it may be more useful to have awareness of the ego. We've all experienced the moment when someone else questions the thing you've produced, or gets involved in a project that is 'yours', or says something passive- aggressive. It's very rarely helpful to have an ego-based response in that situation, no matter how difficult it can be for a moment to swallow your pride and be your 'best self' in a constructive and magnanimous response.

However, being free from concern doesn't mean thinking that everyone else is annoying and wrong all the time. In an ideal world, removing your ego from the situation of work allows you to remove stress and anxiety over 'what this means for me now' (although this is not always possible due to hard financial realities). Moreover, if you are someone for whom concern crops up, then a difficult situation or interaction with a colleague might be exactly the thing that you start to think about just as it's bedtime.

This doesn't mean that we're resigned to putting

ourselves in a position of weakness every time a conflict arises at work. But to aim towards freedom from concern means making a decision. Yes, the high road decision is often the most difficult to take, especially when we're faced with either a stupid person (factually, they do exist) who makes us feel impatient or an annoying person who seems to be getting in our way for no reason (AKA being a jobsworth).

The high road decision (being a team player, thanking others for their feedback and opinion etc.) doesn't provide the ego with the primal bolt of adrenaline in the moment, but it usually results in less post-event concern. Again, in an ideal situation, your manager/boss will see your team-based, ego-less actions and reward them. If that's not where you are then you might need to invest in a 'how to change your job' book.

As a leader, it's a much simpler case. It is vital to remove ego from your actions, as the organisation is a collective group entity and therefore everyone's needs must be seen as equal, alongside the needs of the group as a whole. Put simply, never assume your jokes are as funny as they seem to be.

IN PARENTING

In some places in the world, it is common to heap praise and idealisation onto what is usually the only child of the family. The result of how this manifests itself into adult society are glaringly obvious. Google any definition of narcissism and you can find that a cause of believing oneself to be inherently superior to others is often a result of an upbringing where this was reinforced.

On the other side, criticising a child can obviously have a healthy and very unhealthy side to it. Keeping your child grounded is good, but praising them is also good. Ah, parenting. What we can focus on in this case (relevant to ego) is a particular interaction between parent and child.

This has been my experience with parenting. See what you think. In terms of good parenting and in the closeness of the relationship between a parent and a child, I think there is an important place for the child to be able to mock the parent. I let my children say rude words. I let them call me rude words if it's funny. (in times of mirth they have called me both Dicholas Withycombe and Nick the Dick)

I don't let them have a bad attitude to me, they knew from a young age that 'answering back rudely' was never allowed. Not simply because 'I am the parent and I must be obeyed' nor because I have some kind of ordained greater importance or standing over them, but because it's the right thing to do.

I treat them with respect by making their lives as comfortable as I can, and they return respect by being aware of this and by being nice to me. Less evolved societies see the parent continually reminding the child that they 'owe' the parent back for the work the parent has done, which is not the case with my parenting. I didn't say they 'must respect' me, but they do it by being nice to me.

So, even though they can't and won't simply 'be rude', if we are joking with each other then why can't they call me a dickhead? Because my ego can't take it as I am such an important figurehead of the family? Because other people don't like rude words? This is simply one example, that knowledge of swear words is the same as other topics: if it is going to be experienced, then it's best done in a place of safety and understanding, e.g. the family or the home.

So, good parenting comes from removing your ego from any situation. Of course there is a time for saying 'you have to do this because I give you life, food and shelter', as long as, at some other time, you have clearly explained your motives: it is your responsibility to raise them to be someone who can cope with the world as a sane and organised adult.

Your child will be resentful if they feel that you simply 'say your way must be done' without providing clarity: that your instruction doesn't come from your ego or love of discipline, but your responsibility. Removing the ego also means having the ability to explain this dynamic without emotion, when usually emotions are spiked by the things children do.

It is a difficult balance, but as well as being the authority figure because you have the responsibility, the fuller life experience so far and the will to help them, you must also sometimes be not 'higher up'. Being on the same level as your child and living in the moment – if only in temporary beats such as when playing a game together – has benefits to being free from concern.

Removing your ego also works to give your child the freedom to have their own identity. In these structures, Freud mentions his Oedipus theory, as he always seemed to. I don't believe the Oedipus theory has to be so strict or prescribed – Freud's theory came during a time of parenting in the 1800s and does not relate to the modern, civilised world.

Instead, I think that it is relevant to potential resentment of the father figure. This can happen if the father figure restricts the child's own identity: he basically has an idea that 'my child will be like me', and his ego is then hurt when the child is inevitably different and unique. The father can't comprehend why their child is different, and so he reduces communication, increases criticism and wonders why he is not seen as a King in not only his family but in wider society. This goes into the inevitable development of the crumbling male psyche, which we will talk about later on.

IN ANY SITUATION WHERE YOU ARE WONDERING HOW TO RESPOND

There is a part of more evolved societies that says action is good. If there is a problem then a solution is an action, so let's take an action and that can help. People who are more civilised can sometimes fall into the trap of assuming that all parties are equally as civilised.

The problem there is that taking action can mean 'showing your cards', it can mean making yourself vulnerable. Being vulnerable is unwise if the other party is an a**hole.

Taking action is not always your solution. We'll talk more about later when we look at dealing with the world.

IDENTIFY WHEN YOU ARE BEING PRIMAL AND TRY TO MOVE BEYOND IT

The ego responds to the id being based on more primal urges. While the id is seen as solely primal, it's the urge itself that is primal.

It's primal to want to eat, but the act of eating does not have to be primal, although the way some people do it can be uncouth – yes, I said uncouth – and sometimes I have the feeling that personally I'd prefer to eat in a single dining cubicle so that people didn't ask me a question while I have a mouthful of food. But I digress.

Not being egotistical is clearly good for society – but it's the continued internal conversation between the building blocks of your mind can free you from concern. Being free from concern doesn't mean having some kind of zen-clear mind, nor having a world-dominating will to be superior to others.

Being free from concern might seem like having mint condition mental health, but it's not even about setting oneself that standard. Classically, talking to oneself has been signposted as a state of insanity. I'm here to encourage internal conversation as a route to dissecting and analysing stress and anxiety rather than having an expectation that you can combat it, or shout "leave now, and never come back!". If Smeagol had instead gained the confidence to frankly converse with Gollum then he might be enjoying a walk through Greenwood forest, rather than have plummeted into the lavas of Mordor.

The idea of using your superego means not thinking about 'what this means for me now' or 'how did I look in that situation', but asking yourself how much you even care about it, and whether the issue is relevant in the wider scheme of time and space.

How Setting A Life Goal And Living Without Regret Can Put You On A Pathway To Being Free From Concern

This is about **hope.**

The deathbed theory refers to what you want to be able to look back on when you are 100 years old. When you are older, you will not be able to turn back time and change the things you did: it's a nice perspective to have when making decisions and taking actions in day-to-day life. In the heat of the moment or just in a normal day, we can make decisions out of ego, the influence of hormones and the urge of immediate basic drive or pleasure.

But, no matter who you are, however much success or money you may have; you cannot turn back time. When we make decisions there are many things that we weigh as pros and cons, and they all have a different weight of what we see as better or worse. There are few things worse than regret.

This perspective leads us into thinking about making decisions and taking actions that are not about the short-term or what we want right now.

That can help us to take actions that lead to consequences that we are happy with.

Being happy with potential or real consequences can help us be free from concern.

This is a key piece of the mental puzzle and that's

what this chapter is about: living (behaving, acting, deciding) each day based on what we have decided to be our most important end goal in life. Having some form of goal or result – for later in life – solidifies our self-awareness and identity. This, in turn, forms a mental power of confidence so that no matter what the world brings us, we cannot be knocked off of our path toward it.

HOW TO NOT SET GOALS

Let's have a look at how not to set a goal: the self-defeating phrase
of 'one day'.

It's a common phrase that's said if someone is dreaming of a lofty ambition. They might see anything expensive or desirable – a car, a boat, a luxurious situation or thing – and wistfully comment 'oh well, one day', the idea being that only at some imaginary point in the distant future can it ever be a reality that they could afford or get it.

To me, this seems self-defeating. In my experience, people who say this never get it 'one day'. Instead of being whimsical about success, think about it in real terms.

DON'T 'THINK BIG'

Thinking big or dreaming big is encouraged in the modern world. People say it and assume they will come across as a kind of Oprah meets Tony Robbins meets Tony Stark. OK, I'll think big, thanks. Very thought-leadery of you.

The big thinking is the easy bit. Big planning is the un-natural part.

Talking about being successful or the idea of being successful doesn't come naturally to anxious people (especially good, British people). Of course, social media changed this as it preys on the simple aspects of peer pressure and humans' well-established, ego- driven 'keeping up with the Jones' pattern. As you know, people are keen to show off the 'best' sides of their life, whether it's something expensive, or men trying to look like leaders, or young ladies pointing their anuses at the camera lens while wearing invasively tight yoga clothing, or any person humblebragging on LinkedIn. However, the idea of 'being successful in life' isn't a common part of the real world: our actual conversations.

That might be because 'being successful' is assumed to be something a little conniving, a little soul-less and a little artificial, versus a more meaningful and let's say authentic existence. But what 'being successful' means can still be up to the individual. It could mean raising a family and having a nice house, or it could be living a meaningful and authentic existence. It doesn't have to be the flashy and sick side of other people's social media.

So, what mental hurdles might we need to overcome to look at success? When we grow up, we can often be lost amid a maze of teenage urges;

the need to fit in, the need to be the people our friends and family expect us to be, the need to achieve a set grade in a set subject that we will never ever experience again. Speaking from a developed-world perspective, it's silently assumed that people can finish school, maybe go to University, find someone that 'they really get on well and then fall in love with', marry and have kids and have jobs for a house, a car and holidays. If there's a phrase 'never assume as it makes an ass out of u and me', we could say 'don't assume that you will have a textbook-standard happy life just because society says you will, because life and people and partners can actually be really difficult and you might make terrible decisions without forward planning'. It's less catchy, I admit.

WHAT'S THE REALITY OF 'THINKING BIG?'

Let's look at a reality of success – time and patience. Without massive luck, any success needs planning. I like quotes from unexpected sources, so here's one: I happened to be listening to Liza Minnelli promoting something on TV, and she said "when luck meets preparation, magic happens." This is a great piece of advice when planning your life – which sounds so simple yet few people do it. Perhaps they almost think that planning is 'cheating'? Maybe it seems too easy so it's not worth doing? Maybe they lack the patience? In the world of alleged instant success, a decade can seem like a lifetime to get what you want. Yet, a decade is a realistic time zone for planning success in your life. If you'd planned success a decade ago, you'd be there by now.

So instead of 'think big', if we simply add 'think big and work back', we can see a reality begin to form – the literal (well, metaphorical) steps it takes to get there.

I've found that the simple concept of big picture thinking gets more praise than it deserves – such as when an action is discussed and people say, usually with pride; 'but let's think big'. Yes, that's not difficult – of course having a big picture is good, but it is equally useless without the actions that can get there. How can you define the many, many small steps it will take to get to the goal?

How To Be Free From Concern

Personally, I do not buy into the meaningless yet trendy idea of 'manifesting'. Manifesting is usually something advocated by the same people that think crystal healing is a real thing, and is also happily mentioned by the same Instagram anal-pointers mentioned above. (if you believe this then I am not saying that you are wrong; different opinions are OK)

Thoughts alone do not have mystical powers. It is offensive to suggest that starving masses could manifest themselves out of disaster.

It's more that these points remind me of a kind-of-joke I heard years ago, of a man who prays and prays to God above to win the lottery. He does all the things he's supposed to, but he never wins. He's close to giving up and drops to his knees to finally beg God "why haven't I won the lottery?". At long last, the divine hears him. The clouds part, God appears, and says: "can you at least meet me half way and buy a ticket?"

At this point, I suppose I should say that if you believe in one of the world deities, then you can just pray for things and I wish you all the best with that particular angle.

Instead of the airy quackery of manifesting, fall back to simpler, time-honoured phrases as keys to life: opportunism. Opportunity is the luck part of luck meeting preparation. It doesn't sound especially magical and I wouldn't point your anus at it, but simple 'opportunism' means being as prepared as can be, and learning the 'power' of when to spot opportunities. It means not wasting energy trying to force things – which goes against many modern theories of being successful by being annoyingly pushy (or worse, that simple consistency will result in success, it doesn't) – but identifying where your potential successes actually lie.

Never put yourself in a position of submissiveness by saying that you can achieve something 'one day'. Think big and work back, be patient, prepare and wait for the right opportunities.

Moving From Your Mind And Into Society

Setting Out Your Stall

This is about **empowerment.**
So you have some form of life goal in mind – how can you transform that into being free from concern when interacting with others? This is about the phrase 'setting out your stall'. It doesn't mean that you essentially tell people 'this is what I am doing and if you don't like it then tough'.
It also doesn't mean 'showing people your hand', as we live in a world where that's not always realistically in your best interests. That's not your fault. But I digress.

What you are doing is honestly, politely and descriptively (AKA *authentically* in modern parlance) explaining to people – at the start of whatever relationship is developing, personal or professional – that you live your life a certain way for certain reasons. If they don't like it, that's OK, but the relationship might not work for everyone.
It's about giving yourself not just a 'goal', i.e. a thing to attain, but
a purpose: something that drives you, guides you, lifts you.

I heard 'setting out your stall' explained in a succinct way in a film. It was an American film, thus the word f*ck was used when explaining it.
Just as unexpected as a Liza Minnelli quote, it's a little odd to take life advice from one of Mark Wahlberg's worst films, but I have. It's 'The

Gambler', in which good old John Goodman had a line about 'the f*ck you position'. He explained that before gambling or taking a risk, build yourself into a solid position of impenetrable strength. In the case of the film, he basically advised Marky Mark to first build up 2 million dollars so that he could then go and bet big. But the same theory, applied to life, is a great one.

What it means in life is giving yourself a position which, when challenged, let's you say (at least mentally) 'no, f*ck you, because I'm fine. I don't need you and I don't need this.'

We can look at this in a few different parts of life:

WORK

Of course, the most pragmatic way to have a f*ck you position in your career is financially. Although in wellness it's the mental side that's considered, one simple truth is that the more savings you have, the more reassured you may feel in a job. At the end of the day, you can quit and know that you can fund your life while you look for a new job. If you are yet to build that luxurious position, then at least you can have some mental tools in place that will help in times of challenge. One such tool relates to how you deal with into confrontation or competition; by refusing to be dragged down into it in the first place.

Not entering into confrontation sounds simple – yet if we act on ego and emotion, it's difficult. We're told from when we're a child not to take the bait, not to get into arguments over nothing. But we're also told, as teens and adults, about the competition at work and are programmed to accept certain situations, like going for a promotion and the glamour of competition.

Some things are trumped up as positives in the workplace, like 'taking ownership' for tasks and challenging (arguing) our case and essentially, having feelings about most of what happens. It is seen as good to care are about everything all the time.

If there is a thing in the company that's happening, like a non-work event, discussion, birthday, project/meeting, then relentlessly be your best and care. But also, don't burn out. Take time off. But then come back caring really quite very much thank you.

The general societal message about work is: you should work in your passion, you should show your passion and you should always get involved at work. It's so much emotion. However, that doesn't have to be accepted.

Instead, there may be more success and happiness by taking the position of not competing. This happens by setting out your stall, early on in your job and on an ongoing basis; you aren't someone who 'competes' at work. You put in all your effort but make it clear that this is 'work' and it is not 'life'.

I'm not saying simply 'don't care outright', as that won't work and people will think you are jaded and cynical. Instead, stay positive, friendly, helpful, supportive, praise others, do your work as best as you possibly can. But, if (when) others at work are passive aggressive, make comments you don't like, and other such negative workplace moments, don't respond in kind. Don't send the silly passive-aggressive email at 11pm. Don't compete for something that doesn't matter. Even for a promotion. I'll say it: it's OK not to try for a promotion if you have made the calm and analytical decision that it's not right for you at this time.

Striving to compete and 'hoping for success' can be counter- productive. Failure isn't as great as social media says it is. Do your job in the best way you can, of course. Set out your stall as someone who is friendly and believes in what the organisation is attempting to do. But be clear that you will not be drawn into the emotional battleground of 'what you want to happen' instead always favouring 'what is the best thing for the organisation as a whole'. These are the things that, in an ideal job, will give you success.

If they don't, then perhaps you need to find a better job (i.e. a better boss). But what setting out your stall with the f*ck you position means is that no one can mess with you. Passive-aggressiveness, being pitted against your team-mates rather than alongside them, dealing with the ego and lack of reality from bosses all have the volume turned down. Negativity cannot affect you if you can fall back to this position of confident knowledge: I have my goal, I have my path and I am finding my own success in my own way.

FAMILY LIFE

Indeed, why on Earth would you need anything related to a fall back and a position of confidence in the family? Isn't family life always wonderful, joyous and filled with togetherness and calm? Indeed, indeed.

While 'f*ck you' may seem like overly aggressive language to use relating to family situations, what it is about is a long-term goal. Whether that goal is for yourself or your family unit, thinking long- term in a family setting is important.

Family life can become intense over the very smallest of matters. Big arguments can brew and then erupt over tiny things that later seem laughably petty or are literally impossible to remember. Day to day life with children is mentally challenging, and so is compromise and concern. In this case, it's about having a go-to mantra during times when you feel impatient, ignored or claustrophobic.

Fixing in your mind a long-term goal gives perspective – I've also heard to it being referred as 'zooming out'. Zooming out gives you the perspective that helps you to get over the small, petty stuff. It helps by giving a perspective on the problems that others face and makes you grateful for having family members.

The mental f*ck you position is also good when

outside challenges come to your family. Annoying neighbours, random problems and even miniscule things such as a school receptionist questioning whether your child is really sick enough to stay home; these things can cause large concern. Close and extended family members can be draining in one way or another. Knowing that there is a long-term goal down the road for your family and mentally solidifying why you do what you do is a safe retreat during challenging times.

THE WORLD

The news is often a mix of propaganda, PR, profit-based publishing and click-baited scare-mongering. Social media is essentially the great mental sickness of our time. These forms of information can very quickly create large amounts of concern; anxiety, jealousy, insecurity and so on.

It's difficult but essential to not get caught up with news headlines or social media posts. News headlines are built on attracting attention, and you'd be surprised to know just how much of news is driven by PR agencies and governments, even in supposedly 'free media' nations. That's a topic for another book by another person (or Russell Brand's Instagram videos).

It is known that on social media, everyone seems happy, successful and there are countless aforementioned people who are on LinkedIn "humbly" boasting about an award they won, or others on Instagram pointing their bottoms at you while at the same time writing a caption about mental health and not judging yourself hun.

We are aware of this yet it still tricks us.

It is absolutely crucial, perhaps more than anything, that you ignore social media (and news headlines) when trying to attain good mental health. If you must scroll through for whatever reason, keep firmly in mind that what you are seeing is curated imagery of other people trying to appear successful. The mental f*ck you position should remain on high alert: knowing your own goal so that other's carefully taken, selected and edited images do not affect your reality.

ZOOMING IN

We've looked at setting the big goal (or series of goals) in life by
thinking big and working back.

Another helpful tool relevant to this topic is to zoom back into daily life and the small moments that might otherwise go un- noticed. Savour small victories and small pleasures in life rather than expect the big moments (the ones that are never not posted about on social media!).

The small things in life are often the ones that cannot be destroyed by others. The news may be telling you that another disaster is on the horizon – but the newsreader cannot take from you the joy of a
perfectly boiled egg with a runny yolk. You might have had a difficult work experience but 5 minutes

alone with a perfectly heated, perfectly balanced hot chocolate still feels magnificent. I have used two food examples but there are many others to be found: clear air, blue sky, the changing seasons.

I have also freely used the word perfect in this case without fear of the concern of imperfection, as that's the great thing about small moments: they can be easy to re-attempt and enjoy.

WHAT THE SOLIDITY OF YOUR POSITION GIVES YOU

Clearly understanding your own goal and long-term purpose helps when dealing with daily frustrations. It lets your mind go to a safe place and gives you a perspective.

In times of challenge or stress, give yourself a mental f*ck you position that lets you retreat to a position of mental calm.

Nick Withycombe

Moving Further Into the World

We've looked at the mind. Let's look more into living.

In Appreciation Of Monks

First up is a practical step to reduce concern and, like some of the
points I've made, it leans towards the monk-ish.

Here's one journey of concerned-to-monkishness that has helped me. See what you think.

When I was young, I concerned myself with what to wear.
As a teenager and then in my early twenties, I perused the men's section of Top Man and River Island, fingering through t-shirt sections, hoping to chance upon just the right image or slogan that would clearly signify to females in my age bracket that I was cool. That I was hip. That *I got it.* 'This cool t-shirt will surely secure boobs', I thought to myself.
I did this kind of thing for some time, before realising that I was being an idiot. This is not to say that people who care about fashion or what they wear are idiots: I was being an idiot because I was the one causing myself concern – for no reason.
From that point on, I decided to only wear the same thing – or at least the same type of thing. Plain clothes with no slogan, nor any image, stripe, pattern or diversity or any kind: a uniform. A coat, jumper or t-shirt in black, blue or green. Trousers in grey or dark blue. Comfortable shoes. Cheap versions, bought from supermarkets.

These have saved me huge amounts of money, as

well as hours of clothes shopping and more hours of anguish. Again, if you like clothes shopping and dressing yourself up, then it's not a concern. But if you've ever thought 'oh no, I have nothing to wear' or been concerned at not being able to afford an item, then this can help.

How To Be Free From Concern

This is especially true if you have ever wondered what exact combination of apparel would best demonstrate *who you are* and what you present to the world. Causing yourself concern in this way is odd: no one cares.

The kind of people that you want in your life won't care about what you wear – and the other type are far more concerned with how *they* are demonstrating *who they are* via the clothes they are wearing that day.

I understand that this was easier for me, as a man, because of the way society still regards expectations of how men and women can/should/do look. Even when I stepped out of the norms, it made people uncomfortable (as in they judged me). This includes not wearing a suit in an office and not wearing a fancy suit or tuxedo- type-of-thing at a wedding. Such simple, meaningless deviations from clothing expectation caused alarm. But it was alarm in others

– that's their life experience that they're going to have to come to terms with. This is just one tiny example (or a *microcosm* if you're a thesaurus kind of writer) of how living life free from concern perturbs and disturbs others.

All of us dressing in uniform, like monks, is a scene from a post- apocalyptic movie. I am not advocating the suppression of identity, style or fun. But dressing in uniform, like monks, is also a scene from a temple. Monks do seem free from concern. Which leads us to abstinence – or at least the concept of sex and what it does to our minds.

Now, a man talking about sex in 2022 is risky business, so let the disclaimers begin: I'm not excusing anyone's behaviour related to sex and hormones. I'm not saying that people could have their problems solved by sex. But it's arrogant for anyone to dismiss the notion that their emotions may be led by their hormones. We are still animals and our chemistry prompts us to procreate. A post-orgasmic state is generally free from concern – just for example. I'm also far from the first to openly discuss it, but, again, as a man, I need to disclaim. The Women's Health Instagram can have post after post advocating masturbation, but it would be bizarre and inappropriate for me to say that to women, and men already need little to no further encouragement to lock themselves in a room and have a wank. This does not mean that it's the answer to mental health issues. But it's relevant to our bio-chemical make-up.

SEX IS RELEVANT (there are A LOT OF disclaimers here, so bear with me)

In health and wellness, we talk about emotion, mindset, mood, mentality, psychology, feelings and so on. Well, if you've enjoyed some form of sexual intercourse, then I hope you agree that it feels great!
We can talk all day about eating fruit, doing exercise, communicating openly and the full set of well-being goodness, but an unsatisfying relationship with the topic of sex may cause angst, impatience, sadness, frustration and isolation.

I really need to make it clear at this point that this is a logical, adult discussion. I've brought up this point before (that sex affects mood) and someone replied: "Oh so all a woman needs is a man to make things OK?!"

It may have seemed like a great opportunity to be triggered/indignant, but the actual words I used at that time and am also using now are these: because humans have hormones, sex affects our mood.

I am not 'recommending' anything at all in the world of sex because I am not an expert (I will not write 'sexpert'). Some monks around the world may have purposefully selected celibacy to free themselves from that specific concern of how to obtain sex. I'm not saying do it or don't do it – this is, simply, about awareness.

Awareness and acceptance of how sex can affect us and therefore domino to other people is key to our level of concern.

LISTENING TO YOUR MOOD AND QUESTIONING ITS VALIDITY

In well-being, we're told to tune in to our minds, pause and listen to what it's saying and how we're feeling. This is a great thing to do – but, with acceptance of our moods being swayed by hormones, we can accept that, sometimes, we might be thinking complete rubbish.

Valuing your thoughts is important, but devaluing them can be important too. 'I'm probably being stupid here' is not necessarily a bad thing to think. No one should be so arrogant that they cannot recognise their own mental nonsense.

This comes into play with your hormones as they have such massive control over you.

Put simply: a build-up of certain hormones caused by a lack of sexual activity (either with someone else or by yourself – or if you're lucky then with perhaps a group of people) can make a person act short-tempered, and/or overly flirtatious, among other things.

It's important to know that in the following words, I am not excusing or saying anyone has the excuse to act in certain ways just because of their hormones. But as a man (I can't speak for female behaviour but I imagine there are similarities because we are all human), you might start to take negative actions if you aren't aware that your hormones are controlling you. This can include sending people salacious messages on social media platforms, and/or acting inappropriately in a professional or other environment.

(again, this is not *excusing* such behaviour in any way at all)

Self-awareness can mean recognising this before you might begin to act inappropriately. It means recognising that you are being short-tempered due to your hormones.

(this is not accusing anyone of being irrational due to hormones, but a personal acceptance that our mood may be affected by hormones)

BEING AWARE THAT OTHERS HAVE NOT LISTENED TO THEMSELVES AND ARE ACTING OUT OF CONTROL

Getting control of yourself is great. But others may not have done so, and knowing this helps you to understand why some people are in a bad mood, or in changing moods. It doesn't mean that it gives anyone an 'excuse' to act in a certain way. But at least you have an idea of the potential reasons. (though it might not be their hormones. They might just be born assh*les. They exist.)

SEXINESS AS POSITIVE MOTIVATION

'How can I motivate myself to exercise and stay fit?' is a common question in well-being. There are usually a bunch of suggestions that revolve around mindset. But sex is relevant. I'll say it. Looking at really sexy people can give you the get-up-and-go that you need to make it to the gym or fling yourself around the room at home.

SEXINESS AS SELF-DEFEATING SADNESS-PROMPTING

Being open about reasons for keeping fit is positive. 'I exercise to look good and to therefore increase my chances of physically interacting with someone sexy' is an honest thought. However, I can't help but feel that it's being taken too far in some contexts.

We know it but still can be baited: it's actually unhealthy to look like current social icons. I won't talk about whether it's healthy or not for women to be told by other women on social media to focus quite that much on their bottom size. I won't talk about whether it's healthy for a woman talking about 'not judging yourself' alongside a half-naked photo revealing no fat and the 'perfect' hourglass figure. I won't talk about these things because the world does not need a man talking about women's issues. I will say that it is drastically unhealthy for a man to get the Men's Health cover look with rock hard rippled abs coupling enormous biceps. Being as sexy as Superman or Thor is unrealistic, un-sustainable and unhealthy.

Sex and sexiness are aspects that people need to understand in order to be free from concern. We've talked about a few of them but it's part of the overall discussion of self. Do you have goals related to your physique? How realistic are they? What happens mentally if you get there – or don't?

What is your relationship with your appearance and clothes? Does it ever cause you concern? Could simplifying things help you to remove concern? This is a personal topic where questions are more effective than opinion. Unless there's some appeal in the monk option. You could just go and be a monk. Think about it.

How To Free Yourself From Concern Just Before Bed

Most wellness advice will advocate communication, honest discussion and the like. This can be good but doing this before bed can backfire. What if you don't get the response you would like? Or don't get any response? If you're at the end of a day and are without strong concern, then celebrate the win: you've made it through a day. Having a last check of the news (disaster) or your messages (other people) might start the carousel of mind-questions just as you try to sleep.

Instead, how might you be able to sleep better, feel better and less anxious and more calm? How can you escape the negative side of the outside world? There might be a thousand ways depending on the details of your life. But while this isn't a guaranteed mental elixir, there is one thing that can at least help in some way: pottering.

If you're not sure what pottering means, it isn't gardening, or cooking. I must emphasise at this point that no pots are involved. It's a word used mainly by people in England who were born between 1910 and 1970 (those born between 1970 and 1990 know what the word means, but we don't use it). All it means is: aimlessly going around the house/garden doing small and even meaningless tasks.

Nick Withycombe

This could be: tidying up messy drawers (in a chest of drawers, not your underwear, which would be a different story), organising your toiletries, preparing your clothes for the next day, and so on.

POTTERING GETS YOU MOVING AND LETS YOUR MIND DRIFT TO THE SUBCONCSCIOUS

In the last few decades, younger generations have come to fetishise 'chilling'. Being old before my time, I never quite understood 'chilling' when the term was first introduced around the turn of the new century. I saw/heard young people ask other young people what they did on the weekend (or the Summer and so forth), and the reply was 'just chilled', to which the reply back was 'oh cool'. What was this 'chilling'? Why was it cool? Precisely how did one 'chill'? It took over a decade until I realised that when I was watching TV on the sofa, I had apparently been 'chilling'. Apparently, I was being cool without even knowing it.

I was also curious: these young people did not lead hectic lives. When I first heard the term, it was from students who were working at a cinema part-time. How much further chilled – or worse, 'chillaxed' (2000-2006) – did they really need to be?

These days, people are still being rendered immobile, first by the TV and now by their mobile phones. This self-harming vegetative state has extended all the way up to the older end of Gen X / younger end of baby boomers, as our devices take ever further control of our minds and bodies.

In terms of being free from concern and sleeping

soundly I sometimes find it healthier to disconnect from media, rather than watch media and disconnect from reality. This is because reality is always there waiting for you, so, it's better to come to terms with reality rather than bathe in the fiction of mediocre TV programmes or the presented reality of media.

Connecting to your home is a healthy thing that lets your subconscious mind flow, sorts out ideas and thoughts and takes you away from the negative parts of modern life.

This is the effect of pottering.

Get away from what you've been told is cool: 'chilling' on the sofa and being mildly bored by the nonsense of others. Don't live in a world where everyone is allegedly absolutely successful all the time. Don't browse through TV subscriptions that you don't even enjoy.

Instead, shut the outside world off and do those tasks that are in the back of mind your mind, telling you that they still need to be done. Organise something in the house, write down thoughts (e.g. a to- do list) with a pen and paper, de-clutter the dining table, do some stretching, lay out your clothes for tomorrow, elevate your feet and legs for 15 minutes, talk to a family member, water the plants, take the empty bottle of shampoo out of the bathroom, marinate some food for the next day. The difference can mean going to bed with a clear mind, thanks to the simple time pottering and

How To Be Free From Concern
being connected to what matters.

Nick Withycombe

Living With The Media

I am sure that you do not expect to walk into a place selling newspapers or open your apps and see the headline 'THERE ARE SOME THINGS HAPPENING AROUND THE WORLD NOW BUT 99% OF THEM WILL NOT AFFECT YOU SO HAVE A NICE DAY'.

Businesses that make a profit from concern will continue to create concern. After 18 months of the pandemic, I saw that some newspapers had either run out of new ways to create concern or maybe didn't need to make any effort: one had a frontpage of 'SURPRISE! COVID IS BACK AGAIN!' and one simply had 'FEAR' as the opening word.

In terms of social media, as we know, there are dangers. There is also a lot of #mentalhealthawareness out there. Too much? Possibly. There are some accounts that seem to offer supportive advice and thoughts, but even those seem dangerously wallowing in self-pity rather than positivity. There is one in particular that seems to insist that 'adult life is cleaning the kitchen' and with a ceaseless 'I didn't do anything today because I am pathetic' outlook. It moves from empathy into enabling others to dig their own hole of helplessness, rather than commit to finding a way out.

I don't find it realistic to delete apps and never look at news at all, but I never watch news on TV.

How To Be Free From Concern

Every time I read headlines or articles, I think about the various government scandals that were big news before they were replaced by the new "crisis" or "disaster" that has taken their place instead. Having worked in PR agencies before, I think about whether this article or review was simply placed there, either for a fee or by an editor who received a nice gift.

That's it. It's that simple. The sane choice is between looking at news headlines and wondering why they are there – or not looking at them at all. They are not informing you, they are concerning you.

Not engaging, not voting, not having argumentative debates with family members; these are things that others frown upon. The purpose of saying this is to prepare you for a confused or critical response from others when you explain to them that you don't watch the news.

However, their own blind hysteria should not be a factor in your own choice of media consumption. This is just a note on a potential social consequence of you taking your own choices and deciding how you want to consume outside information. This is one example of a consequence of being free from concern: bizarrely enough, it can make people feel uncomfortable.

Whether that's due to their subconscious jealousy of your mental comfort, or their lack of understanding about why you are living in a certain way; being untroubled can confuse others. It's that animal part of our brain that finds comfort in homogeny. If a predator gets into the sheep field, all the sheep huddle together. There's rarely one sheep off to the side thinking 'I refuse to live scared and I can probably trample that fox anyway'.

'Why is that person untroubled? What, do they think they're better than me or something?' These are the kind of dim-witted, weak and frankly ovine thoughts that may be had by others who see you smile in adversity.

Envy and confusion can be consequences of success. Living free from concern is a mental and spiritual success that lifts you up. There are those people who feel unable to rise to your level, so they aim to achieve parity by dragging you down to theirs.

Fortunately, the response of inaction is described later on, and is one to turn to should you encounter a confused flock or individual who bleats in your direction.

How To Be Free From Concern

More on living in the world and going
against what you're told

Nick Withycombe

Going Against The Grain

In techniques of reducing concern, mindfulness is mentioned. Mindfulness is simple and good. It's basically awareness, one of the important traits that we've already discussed.

Mindfulness is another way of saying stop and think about what you are doing. Actions have consequences, so what are the consequences of your actions in life? Just like kids are told to count to 10 before replying if they feel angry, mindfulness means noticing what is happening rather than letting it pass by. Pause for a moment before taking actions.

This is great, but anything can go too far. For the concerned amongst us, being too mindful, too aware, too questioning, can lead us to go round in circles. Hence the timeless phrase 'too much of a good thing'. Old phrases last generations because they are very accurate.

Mindless living can also be good. Look, I've listed a few reasons
why!

MINDLESS EATING

What would tantalise me? Thrill me? What would really set the tone for current life? What are people eating/photographing on social media? These are questions that can drive your relationship with food toward fat, sugar and stress. Picking 'just the right' restaurant that will thrill your life and really let people know on social media that you are living it right up is also too much hard work. People who do not feel anxiety may find this bizarre. How can we let something as simple as eating cause us angst? Because we are special.

I have found it helpful to simplify eating. Not always, sometimes just on weekdays, or for periods of time. Quickly frying/roasting/steaming 'some sliced vegetables' and 'some protein' and a carbohydrate with some herbs and then adding a couple of favourite condiments is a very healthy, filling and stress- free way to enjoy a meal without any emotional baggage attached. I don't eat it 'mindfully', thinking about each grain of brown rice. Safe in the knowledge that it's healthy and filling, my mind can drift into a subconscious flow state.

MINDLESS WEEKENDING

Watching TV and going for a walk and doing mindless eating and tidying the house is a great way to spend a weekend. And when colleagues or anyone asks "how was your weekend", don't say you did nothing, say it was "great!". It is great to not have the hassle of creating unforgettable memories or precious, rosy-cheeked times just because it's a Saturday and Sunday. Don't even say you 'binge watched' something, because that's still some kind of pseudo-cool tick-box that causes people to unnecessarily reference Netflix. Use mindless, non-socially approved wording and enjoy the power of individuality.

Nick Withycombe

MINDLESS PARENTING

Tired parenting can be better. You know the moment where the other parent contradicts what you've said to your kid – in front of the kid? And you get all ego-fueled and uppity that your parenting word has not been seen as sacred? That usually happens with the first child. By the time you're in the baby years of the second, you lack the energy or spirit to care that your golden word has been muddied. You are too tired to care.

This is great because you won't start a meaningless argument with your spouse, you'll just lightly shrug your shoulders and go back to munching your steamed vegetables.

MINDLESS WORKING

If you are doing things and then people pay you to do those things, then it's a wonderful mindless win. While others are keenly posting about their new job or award or recent project that their employer did – don't. As they are 'excited to be a part of' and 'delighted to announce' and commenting that there's a 'great line up' for the next webinar (or Hybrid Forum, Symposium etc) and virtue-signaling the life out of whatever is trending that day and that day alone, quietly think to yourself that you are greatly enjoying the money that your job has provided.

If others race to sign up to the 'work thing that's not a work thing but will score you points with management', then do your contracted tasks really really well but don't stress about bottom- licking endeavours. This also comes back to setting out your stall, as mentioned previously.

MINDLESS LIVING

Maybe go for a run, maybe don't. Maybe choose a roasted vegetable dinner, maybe have noodles. If another driver over-

takes, swerves in front of you or does something idiotic, don't put your foot down or compete with them for nothing. If a friend or family member talks politics then politely nod along. These inactions mean that when the moment stops, you don't have any left-over second-thoughts, angst, regrets or emotional stickiness. We'll talk about inaction in the next section.

MIND-BODY CONNECTION

Mindfulness suggests that you need to sit and think deeply. Don't!
Move your body instead.

How can mindlessly moving your body transform your mind? Never think of yourself as beyond science. You may be feeling stressed, but that doesn't mean that gravity doesn't apply. Never assume that your physical state is not affecting you.

How can going for a walk directly affect the

problem that's making you worry? Maybe it won't, but your mindset is made up neurons and cells and things. It's not made of stone. It can change. Going for a walk can divert your mind into a more subconscious, less worried status wherein you are able to mindlessly gain a new perspective.

Inaction: Specifically Looking At How To Respond To Difficult People

"How can I react? What should I do?"
Here's why a counter-intuitive response of 'nothing' can be best
for your well-being.

There are traits that you will have heard being labelled as positive. 'Being positive' is seen as positive. So too is being open, as is looking for solutions, finding a middle ground, taking on challenges, learning, winning, failing.
You've seen so much of this online (particularly the fetishisation of failing), and so you might think that these are good actions or reactions.

But not always.

Sometimes, 'doing nothing' is excellent. It can be a powerful
response, and it can be a helpful method to follow.

Doing nothing can take many forms. When someone says something rude or instigating, don't reply. When a colleague or boss messages you on the weekend, don't reply. If you feel dissatisfied or bored, do not 'act' as the first solution. If someone is trying to attract/distract you or get your attention, do not give it. It's at this point that I should make disclaimer – I'm not encouraging deviousness or persuading you to 'not be a good person'. Some of this will seem counter-intuitive for good people. And it's not telling you to remain closed to all people and situations! But in my experience, doing nothing can be the best option in a number of occasions.

HERE ARE SOME OF THOSE OCCASIONS

General life:
People who have grown up in civilised societies might assume that, as adults, we can all act and the situation will improve and turn out well. We may believe that positivity, openness and a good frank interaction will win the day.

In reality, if you're dealing with someone who is just difficult, then you might open up, have what you think is a genuine and positive interaction – and then be further hurt by the person using your openness against you down the line.

Online life:
'It'll be this accurate comment that really settles the argument!', said many people in their heads. On an online platform, in an email chain or the like, there has never, ever been one comment that really 'wins' the argument and shows everyone who's right. It's all equally infantile.

And when you see something seethingly, annoyingly incorrect that someone else has posted somewhere, 'righting their wrong' by making your own poignant comment only adds fuel to their post.

How To Be Free From Concern

In an argument with your partner:

This possibly needs a longer explanation but the summary is that if you want to be in a long-term relationship with someone – let's just say marriage as it's the current majority global format of this – then in normal life, friction happens. And if you want it to work, then you are going to have to choose to occasionally not say the thing that you want to say.

At times, we have a choice of letting the situation calm down or making it worse. We're told by the media and so forth that relationships must be 100% honest. 'Communication is good'. This does not mean that, during an argument, you need to go back into the imaginary filing cabinet of past misdemeanours and wrongs that your partner has allegedly committed.

With a hopeful assumption that your partner is human, sometimes apply a verbal filter for their sake – and yours.

AT WORK

Work can be such a strange environment. It's a group of people whom you are often thrown in with randomly. You are 'supposed to' get quite close, be open and share who you are. But you are also expected to continually show your best side. Turn up at the office well-groomed, be nice, not have any failings or cynicisms and laugh at every joke made by someone who is in a more senior position. If you're unfortunate, then some of those around you can be difficult. Those more senior in the hierarchy can be egotistical. There can be passive-aggressive (or just aggressive) comments, emails, and the tactical weekend message. From a boss, this might start with 'don't reply now, but…'.

Between colleagues, it never pays to engage in email nastiness. No one has ever made a considered response to an email argument/accusation that results in the other person saying 'oh yeah, you're right, sorry'. It only leads to more baiting and silliness.

Work is distinct from other situations, where it can be possibly easier to do nothing – otherwise known as taking the high road. Taking the high road, in my experience, is always the best thing to do. Old expressions are truisms – often centuries old – because they work. Take the high road and 'don't go down to their level' are two phrases that provide excellent imagery of what you need to do and why.

But at work, it's about your income, your livelihood. We've talked about removing ego and setting out your stall. Sometimes, grinning and bearing it is a reality that adults need to experience. A hypothetical action in your head is a good test of what the responses might be. If you said the words, what might be the consequence? Any response to your action might be worse than if you'd have done nothing at all.

Social Concepts Of Age And How They May Concern You

Don't think of yourself as an adult in your 20s – or maybe at any age.

Sorry to trigger! This mere suggestion may trigger some in their 20s, in that outrage that young people have if anyone suggests that they are not a completed human being (or that having more life experience is a good thing).
It's a bit 'OK boomer', although being in my early 40s I'm not sure 'OK Gen X' works quite as well.

But the problem with being in your 20s in some societies: you've been socially groomed into thinking that once you get to around 22, you're an adult. You have finished education, you move out (or should at least desperately want to move out) from home and are ready to start a relationship that may very well lead to marriage and creating new humans and staying together forever because you like each other lots. Oh also your entire life of employment might have been defined already for you, so keep going and get more promotions and money later.

It's essentially saying; 'although you're completely new to the
adult world, make all of the seminal life-decisions right away!'.

It's not that anyone in their 20s simply 'knows less' or is immature – this is not someone who is older saying that 'the young are bad'. It's about not feeling obligated to be an adult, not feeling the need to commit to anything and most of all it's about pressure and how you deal with it.

DON'T FEEL THE NEED TO SAY YOU'RE IN LOVE OR COMMIT UNTIL YOU'RE OLDER

One of the most ridiculous things that people do in their teens is say they are in love. A teenager who says they're in love would refute this. They really know love. They know other teens don't – but they do. Someone in their 20s who hears a teen say they are in love would think it's silly – while being sure that, because they broke the age 20 threshold, their love declarations are now entirely accurate. This is how divorce happens. Well, one reason (the other reason is that marriage is an unnatural concept, but this isn't about that).

In some so-called "developing" societies around the world, people are heavily pressured into marriage – and they hate it. It causes enormous damage to mental health, both in the process and as a consequence in life. If you're not living in such a society then you may not need to essentially force yourself into marriage just because you really like each other at that moment in time.

DON'T EXPECT THAT YOU KNOW 'WHAT YOU WANT TO BE' ALREADY

Listen to older people who say 'I always thought that I would like to…' do a different job other than the one they did for years. The 20s is a great age to try different roles if possible – while keeping in mind that not everyone else is so completely successful as they profess. It's a great age (as is any) to travel. However:

DON'T EXPECT THAT THE WORLD IS HOW YOU'VE BEEN TOLD IT IS

Every year there are several cases that you read on the news – a young person was the victim of violent crime while travelling the world. They've been brought up in a safe bubble of A Town in A Safe Country, and they think that people around the world are either 'all the same really', or just nice and friendly (when being paid tourist cash). So, they entrust their safety with a stranger on the beach of some exotic destination elsewhere on the planet, sometimes at night after drinking alcohol. This is a terrible decision and not a logical one. #travelsafelyanddonttruststrangers isn't 'cool' (OK Gen X) but it's good for your well-being.

Also the above stays relevant in all decades of age.

The Really Annoying 'Comfort Zone' Analogy

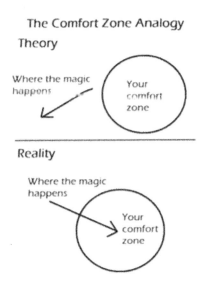

It's possible to be well aware of the real problems on Earth – yet still feel infuriated by an analogy. The language of 'where the magic happens' prompts visions of men with goatees, knowingly nodding while they say 'where the magic happens'. As they say it, they ripple their eyebrows and gurn out smarmy facial expressions that show that – above all – they totally, like, GET, where the magic *actually* happens. No, they MAKE magic happen. They wake up at 5am and go on a 10-mile run and then tell everyone how productive it makes them feel to be incredibly tired by the afternoon.

How To Be Free From Concern

As you can tell, #theinfuriationisreal. That superfluous hashtag was a self-aware one, btw. I do not have a goatee.

This is just another strategy of people – people who want to create an appearance of being the maverick, the risk-taker, the wildcard bungee jumper with the photos to prove it. Their assurance of having found success by not only stepping out of but by then specifically denigrating the comfort zone might trick you into thinking that it is true. Maybe it is – but I have not found that to be the case, not in my experience nor observing that of others. In terms of being free from concern, the usual comfort zone analogy is especially incorrect.

I see the comfort zone as a place where I do what I am good at. I am comfortable when I do what I am good at. It makes other people feel comfortable. I can practice it, I can get better at it. I experience the comfort of confidence, accurate expectations and consequences. You might even say that I experience the magic of comfort and joy, along with financial success in relation to working life.

When I think of where I have stepped out of the comfort zone, I experienced stress and anxiety. This doesn't mean that I don't try new things. It doesn't mean that I dislike variety or that I have only lived in the same village or only eaten shepherd's pie from a young age. Variety is the spice of life – a true analogy that can be said normally.

Nick Withycombe

To be free from concern, to feel safe and comfortable, be 'in the zone'. The comfort zone.

How To Be Free From Concern

It helps to be aware that those who champion discomfort as some guaranteed pathway to growth might be fibbing. They might be re- posting that same tired visual from the comfort of their home, feeling all snuggly in their jim-jams that they accrued through the standard activity of regular employment. They may even have had their pyjamas bought, paid for and gifted to them by another person. Which brings us on to the iceberg analogy. Analogy is my trigger word, you can tell.

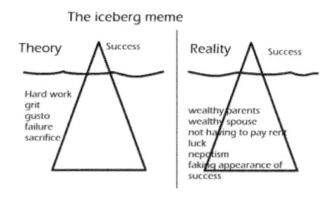

The iceberg meme

This isn't to diminish the people who have earned their own success through hard work and so on. But the 'iceberg of success' meme can potentially be damaging if it makes you compare your reality with the claims of others.

It can be healthy to look at other people who have found the kind of success that you want, and use it as motivation. But it can also be unhealthy to think that 'everyone else' has used long-nights, *grit* and wily street-smarts to find success - and you haven't.

People on social media, or anywhere, are very keen to show their 'success'. But you don't always know the story behind it. It might have been a meritorious journey or it might just be something they did without having the stress of paying rent (for example).

This isn't about judging people for how they got what they have; but about how they choose to portray that, and what it means for you. The purpose is: realise that you define what success means to you and do not to compare it to how anyone else claiming that they reached theirs.

TO CONCLUDE

The boiled down version

WHEN THINGS
ARE GOING WELL

Say you don't have a particular concern and things in life are all going well. You have full realisation and awareness of your goals, your interactions with others, your consumption of society and media. You're great! But you still feel concerned. Sigh.

This is just the way it's going to be sometimes. #mood.

So far we've had, quite literally, a book about freeing yourself from concern mentally. But when you don't want to think any longer, here are some actions to take when you have a lingering cloud for literally no reason:

WORK WITH CHILDREN AND ANIMALS

Children and animals are generally free from concern. Be like them. Well, in some ways. Play a board game with your kids/relatives and gladly descend into the level of the silly and the domain of the easily-fascinated. Go for a walk in nature and step outside of the constructed world of mankind.

WAIT FOR TOMORROW

More acceptance! Accept your mood and don't fight it. Accept grumpiness today and plan something, anything, to give yourself tomorrow.

BE INSPIRED BY YOURSELF

When get a feeling of malaise, gloom or despair, it can sometimes simply be through boredom. If other people don't seem to be helping with this, then take action to inspire yourself. Do anything creative. Make a plan!

TAKE OFF THE ARMOUR OF CONCERN

Of course, normally, we can't simply let go of concern. However, sometimes we get used to it. It's our habit, our norm. It's even possible to wear concern as a badge of honour. Either 'I worry, so I am good' or a bizarre kind of attractiveness to worry as a shield: as if by being worried, you are telepathically deterring bad things from happening.

Even if we know how, it can still make it difficult. Are you sure that the wires are really disconnected if I take off the explosives I've had tied to me for so long? Take off concern and put on awareness instead.

ACCEPT BIOLOGY

'I am probably only worrying because my brain structure is causing it.'

How To Be Free From Concern

Enhanced concern has been gifted to us by our ancestors. Labelling your concern as 'this funny thing that a part of my brain does' lets you use another part of your brain to remind you of logic and sanity.

It's OK to accept that your mood might be because of your hormones, or your caffeine/sugar/stimulant intake.

Seeing yourself as one animal on the planet during one moment in time can help to bring perspective to your concerns.

USE ANXIETY TO EMPOWER YOURSELF

We've talked about inaction, but sometimes it's time to stroke your goatee and make some magic happen. If you are anxious about something not working out, or of someone getting in there first (whatever that may mean) or of losing out on an opportunity: turn that concern into action. Take control of the 'what if' and the consequences.

WALK

Put one foot in front of the other. For a very long time.

That's the final recommended action in this section. Maybe you shouldn't do this if it's midnight and you're reading in bed. But when it's not weird to do so, go for a nice long walk and see if it helps you to be free from concern.

Nick Withycombe

How To Be Free From Concern
Things You Can Do

Actions, exercises and stuff.

Breathing

Some people swear by specific breathing exercises to feel calm, centred and with a reduction of anxiety. There are many of these on YouTube that you can and maybe should try, just to see if you like it or not.

I do not. I don't find it helpful to specifically sit or be in one place,
with my eyes closed, focusing on my breath.

However, I have found a way that putting focus on breathing can have some kind of effect. So, if the 'close your eyes and don't move and breathe' effort doesn't work for you, then you can still have a go at the same focus – while you're doing something else.

It could be cooking or doing something round the house, or even just looking out of the window. You can also try to focus on just three, or five, or ten single breaths. Control inhalation and control exhalation. That's it.

Removing the hoopla and ceremony from the action helped me to put in perspective how simple it was; so when the noise in your head becomes jumbled, take five breaths – even while doing other things. There's no need to sit in the stock photo, cross-legged yogi pose. Gain control over a few breaths and gain a very small but noticeable benefit of focus.

Meditating

The same theory applies to meditating as it does to breathing. You don't need to find a calming playlist or dim the lights or listen to someone 'guiding' you through something.

Of course, you can if you want!

But it feels too structured and po-faced to me.

Instead, I realised that when I was eating alone, I was basically meditating. No one has an authority on what meditating is or isn't. It does not have a single, perfect definition. Yet, even the big names in the meditating head space will tell you that you "need" to sit and close your eyes and so on. They say you can "only feel the benefits" by maintaining regular practice.

Refuse to be told words such as "only" and "need to".

I believe that simply giving ourselves any amount of time and space can help us to achieve meditation. Eating alone, sitting in your car waiting, walking, or any activity in which your mind is free to wander; these moments can be spaces where you consciously press pause on other things and allow yourself a meander through the subconscious.

The same concepts can be applied as traditional meditation; such as not rejecting thoughts, not being distracted by noise but allowing them to happen and being aware of them without judgement. Just give yourself a moment to reflect on the day, the week, your thoughts and feelings.

Play Time Travel

Being in the present can be helpful, but so can moving your mind through time. You know those moments where we talk about what we did in the past – and how with hindsight we might have done things differently?

When we look back at the decisions we've made and the way we lived in the past, we feel wiser, calmer and less attached to immediate emotional or egotistical gain. We can think about how we may have done things differently; so try applying that same mental methodology to the present.

It can also be a helpful way to think about the opportunities you have now, so that when you are a decade down the road, you don't see that you had an opportunity to do something to benefit your life – but didn't take it.

If you were ten years in the future, what would you say to your current self?

How would your future self feel about the way you are living now? Ten years from now, would you look back and think 'if only I had/hadn't…'?

Fixate And Punctuate

We all need something to look forward to – sometimes, in adult life, we forget that. It's easy to be caught up in days and weeks rolling by. The effect of having something fixed in the calendar ahead means that there is a subconscious punctuation of time.

Instead of focusing so much on the success of the current daily/weekly routine, make sure that there's always something down the road; anything that can bring joy, no matter how small that may be. The immediate moment of uncertainty can be replaced by a mental glance forwards and a reminder that there is good stuff on the way.

Fixating on a long-term goal is what we talked about previously. Personally, I see it as the most powerful force of positive mental health. There are no rules to this. You can make it something that seems ridiculously big – and still be OK with a knowledge that you won't get there. You can make it something that is very achievable
– the purpose is to agree with it in your mind. Whatever it is, saying it to yourself is important; it gives a purpose not only to life in general but your daily decisions.

As mentioned, give it a timeline too. It could be moving to a bigger home in ten years, or it could be traveling the world or visiting a very specific place or changing your appearance (it's your choice!) or creating some kind of 'empire' (whatever that means for you) or helping others or making the world a better place.

Thinking big and working back puts you on a path. Being on a path means a sense of identity, worth and purpose. It's not just that this gives you a robust consciousness but a sense of purpose emanates.

It somehow communicates itself to the world. Other people sense an aura of confidence and individuality which can cause a reaction of respect and security. Their feeling that you are 'on your way' and living your own life gives people comfort that (1) you aren't going to ever be in their way and (2) you have gone through a spiritual journey already and you have been able to make some sense of human existence.

You've cracked the code of existentialism.

Nick Withycombe

Play With Your Assumptions

Always feel free to have a mental (and physical) play! There has been an emphasis here on goal setting and its magnificent power to solidify a robust confidence of spirit. But always feel free to shift it around and mentally manipulate it – if only for shits and gig's.

Am I assuming I like this? Do I think I like this because of any nature versus nurture formative influence? What would happen if I just went in a completely different direction?

The goal setting doesn't have to be a final decision. It's your choice. By giving yourself the freedom to do whatever the shitbollocks you want at any point in either writing a book or living your life, then go ahead and do it and the rest of the world can go spin on a dick.

Transmogrifying Niceness Into Boldness

I just really wanted to use the word *transmogrifying* once in this book. If I'd just dropped it into a sentence then I feel that I would have had to have explained it in brackets, such as "transmogrifying (that means magically turning one thing into something better)".

However, explaining to your readers what the complicated words mean is patronising. Oh poo, that's what I'm doing now!

As I harped on about in this book's introduction, we can assume that you are a good, nice person. Let's make that assumption. I want the reader to be nice. That's you. Hi. I like you. Anyway, getting on with the point:

People who experience concern might be labelled (by society) as shy, meek, lacking in confidence. Maybe even labelled as weak, submissive, unsure, confused. Losers, in other words.

But we are not losers.

We just care.

We consider.

We think. A lot.

Nick Withycombe

Then we think too much.
Vastly too much.
Then we get concerned.

Then, even if we have a strong exterior, we have an internal

tempest (that means uproar) of repine (that means worry, discontent or fret).

Because we have these negative feelings, we might think that we're bad, we're losers, we're not confident, we can't do well in certain situations.

I say no more! How can we reverse that damaging chain of thought? How can we magically turn our repine into power? How can we find confidence? How can we press one button and make the font of our personal expression **bold**? That last one might not quite have worked but you get the point.

What about trying this as a thought process?!:

Yes, I worry.

I am aware of this. I do it because I care.

My awareness and my concern make me intelligent and good.

I want the world to be a good place and I care for my fellow human.

I am one human on Earth who sees things for how

How To Be Free From Concern

they are and wishes for a better world.

More people should care like I do.

I am something of a leader. I am something other people should aspire to be.

I have a superpower.

I'm like Neo in The Matrix.

I am completely fucking amazing and I will use my superpower to go out into the world with awareness, purpose and vision. GO ME.

Mic drop. Boom. Cue the theme tune. (I choose *Baywatch*)

Look At Your Actions

'I want A – but I keep doing B'. Maybe you really want B? Ah B. Good old B.

'I want to lose fat but I keep eating fatty food' – maybe you actually want to eat fatty food more than you want to lose fat?

'I want to be in a relationship but I can't find the right person' – maybe you don't want to be in a relationship because other people are too annoying to be worth living with?

'I want to get a qualification but I keep wasting time watching TV'
– maybe… may be… may B be the answer?

I don't know, but it's the old phrases that last; actions speak louder than words. The urge, the want and desire can be so strong when they arrive. But then they leave and you're left with yourself again. Nothing against so-called self-improvement – but by whose definition of what improvement is?

The idea of doing something is nice, but it can be often be provoked by peer pressure (AKA Fear Of Missing Out, social expectations etc.) and, if we discontinue the desire then we can feel as though we failed. We feel as though we lack the socially praised traits of being motivated, inspired, having grit and gusto, doing wonderful things. Making the magic happen. Tending to our goatees.

How To Be Free From Concern

We can feel concerned by the discrepancy between our own thoughts and actions.

During these times (now, more than ever), question the thought rather than assume its priority over your action. Not just why you think it but also how realistic is it and what would be needed to make it happen.

It's not about whether you want the result: do you honestly want the actions it takes to get there?

It's OK to say no.

Nick Withycombe

Night And Day

For some of us, concern is a nocturnal companion. This gives me a chance to be a little vocabularistic and say that diurnal (that means daytime) thinking can often be more beneficial.

It might really be that simple. If you are fretting in the night then you need the saner part of your brain to speak up: wait and see if you feel like fretting in the morning. (if you are actually experiencing delirium or serious sleep loss then again, this is what medical professionals and healthcare are there for: seek help)

Sometimes there are simply real-life concerns that concern the concerned. But at other times, the clarity of daylight is the humble tonic to strengthen sane thought processes against the skittish. I've played the insane nighttime 'what if' game many times – and by 'game' I mean convincing myself of completely ridiculous and scary outcomes that, in reality, had no chance of ever materialising.

The next day always brings lucidity of thought and a return to reason.

Save yourself by accepting this bizarre timing of logical consciousness – that's why people say 'sleep on it' and why the morning has always been viewed as a time of sacred simplicity. When the night terrors arrive, tell them that you'll speak to them in the morning.

Time For Action

Earlier on we looked at the power of inaction. This is more relevant when thinking of reacting, or being distracted. If your concern is about a larger situation – let's say poverty or famine – then act!

I remember one particular occasion when I happened to be living in Asia. (you can imagine another author dropping that into a book in order to seem, like, totally cool; but I am trusting that you trust me not to have done that here. Also why do people thinking doing things like 'living in Asia' is cool? There are already billions of people doing that. I digress.)

I was speaking to North Americans in a public house (they called it a 'bar').

As usual with such people, the topic turned to politics and the discussion became fixated upon which one of us at the table was left or right wing. Apparently, we need to be defined. Some of them were proud to say that they were left wing, with the general hint that this was because they cared about equality and such.

They assumed that I was right wing, because I am a white man. I corrected them that I am white because I am English and not all English/British people define themselves with a segmented wing. Because their assumption slightly annoyed me, and I felt like being a bit British for a minute, I questioned those who claimed to be left wing. 'Simply walking down the road and having left wing thoughts does not help your fellow human', I stoutly opined, bristling with Britannic flair and erect with confidence. (if you are not British then I should explain that I didn't necessarily disagree with them, but it is an innate part of my culture to play Devil's advocate and debate things just for the fun of provocation)

An uncomfortable silence descended and with my fun over I retreated to the standard public posture of my country's people; generalised reticent brooding.

The point is not to go out and save the world. Nor to make good deeds public – god knows that there are already enough people happy to signal their virtues on social media. But if the state of something is causing concern then simply 'doing your bit' can be an answer. Every little helps. As mentioned previously, peer pressure can make it seem as though other people are continually achieving, disrupting, graduating and magic-making.

It's not about being the next Greta Thunberg – Greta Thunberg has that one covered for some time yet. The media you consume is a business that earns more money by reminding you of what you're concerned about. You don't have to end the entire problem – instead, find comfort in contributing any small amount of energy in the right direction and, in doing so, you may be able to tick it off the mental list of concern. And then it's

How To Be Free From Concern
straight back to reticent brooding, be off with you!

Nick Withycombe

Research Who Made You

It's not your fault. That line was said by Robin Williams in the film *Good Will Hunting* and, as you know, he had some mental issues of his own. But it was a memorable line, and one that you can apply to yourself.

Older generations always tell younger generations that they lack a sense of responsibility and blame their parents too often. Older generations generally find it difficult to accept that the world has changed from when they were young. Blame and non-acceptance are rife in intergenerational dynamics.

I am of the opinion that it is the fault of the parent. That doesn't mean the parent is bad or actually 'at fault', because we're all human anyway (and all have parents!). Of course we don't do things perfectly! The good thing is that we strive to improve and I believe the world is slowly but continually a better place.

That smidgen of optimism isn't the point though: the point is that you are a result of nature and nurture. Of course, you have free will real free will, not like alleged Christian free will where you are told that your choices are freely your own but He already knows what you're going to choose anyway and then has the eternal heaven/hell booking planned for you. When I say 'research who made you', I don't mean some male kind of spirit-y thing that made every atom in the universe and to whom footballers pray when they step on the field of play, apparently saying "I know there are starving diseased kids and stuff but can you just let me play well in this game for an hour? Thanks!". I don't mean the male kind of cloudy dude who supposedly hates gays but also created 'free will' and also sees everything, resulting in Him disapproving of gays but also literally watching every gay experience that there has ever been and ever will be on Earth. I don't mean that.

I mean:

Do what research you can into your parents, their parents and the whole extended family. If you're lucky this could mean asking a grandparent, but somehow you can try to find out who these people were. Where did they come from, what work did they do, what quirks did they have, what life did they lead?

Knowledge of what genetic cocktail has brewed your neuro noodle helps you to accept whatever you mentally cook up each day. I, for example, learned that even my grandparents' parents were adventurous, they liked to explore and move to new regions, sometimes even doing so to benefit their children. This means that I can see why I bear the anxiety of a concerned parent.

But more than knowledge, I find that it helps me to strive to improve. I can learn about any difficulties my elders faced, I can analyse their shortcomings with an empathetic and compassionate eye, and I can consider both how I can improve my own mindset and then furthermore that of my own children.

In doing so, I can see a line of better well-being thread through my genetic lineage and hope that I have played my part in upgrading the existence of my particular genetic pool.

That perspective lifts me out of the day-to-day and gives me the will to fix any of the weaker genetic gifts that have been passed on to me. This replaces concern with the pursuit of happiness and the purpose to live well – not to secure my bestowed eternal resting place but to take Earthly actions that can benefit real future generations to come.

Replicate Confidence

Just because we are concerned doesn't mean we aren't sometimes extroverts, sometimes pioneers, sometimes leaders, sometimes ultra-confident. We just have our moments, that's all.

So, what if – get this – when the anxious moment arrives we can somehow take our brain out of that and place it into the moment of positive light?

Here's an example!

What if you have to do something you aren't comfortable with such as public speaking, or speaking up of any kind?

Well, if you have children then you are the leader in the dynamic. There is power in being a parent as it somehow gifts you with the ability to feel completely sure about something:

There is no grey area or worry in your own drive to be the carer – to even defend your family with your life should the need arise. That's a complete confidence, a type of situation wherein you feel fearless.

What if you could harness that fearlessness when you need it?

In this case, that could be somehow imagining that your kids were present at the moment of public speaking: so you took on 'Mum mode' or 'Dad mode' at the time, feeling surety of power.

Other such moments could be anything: when you do a favourite hobby, when you listen to a particular song, when you are with a particular person.

Try to replicate the positive moments and insert that mode into your mood when a challenging thing presents itself. It might not work immediately but it is a road to direct your worried mind down when you aren't sure where else it might go.

Find Any Kind Of Win-Win

Impending doom and annoyance with sub-optimal conclusions are the natural home of the concerned.

However, you may be able to find some comfort in convincing yourself that there is a silver lining to the weighty cloud – no matter how illogical it may be.

That's the key point: it doesn't have to make particular sense and it won't make the 'what if the bad thing happens' easier, but once you look at what you may gain as part of the result, then your brain can cling on to something other than the negative.

For example: what if a comet smashes into the Earth? Well at least I won't have to worry about paying the electricity bill. Or: what if there's another pandemic? At least I can do all the things I didn't get round to last lockdown. Or not.

Post-apocalyptic movies are popular because they provide us with the fantasy of not needing to pay bills anymore. Use that psychological dynamic to be a giddy optimist. You know the mad people on top of the tower in alien movies, holding signs that say "Welcome to Earth" or "Beam Me Up"? That's you that is.

Nick Withycombe

The Relativity Of Concern

If you're searching for a way to become immediately unpopular – then look no further! Telling someone that they shouldn't feel bad because other people have worse problems is a great way to make them hate you.

So, I'm not going to say that. Well, not precisely – I'm going to re- word a very similar idea over two paragraphs.

Of course, during a peak or a trough of difficulty, such a comment is unlikely to help. But it's not really about the direct comparison it's about zooming out and looking back down at yourself as one person in time and space, relative to other people.

If you look at some people who are really suffering (let's say homeless or hospitalised), then it doesn't mean you are simply dismissing your own issues. Instead, reminding yourself of what capacity, abilities and opportunities you have available to help yourself can do just that: help yourself to take a positive decision or action. Seeing others deal with it should allow you to take inspiration from their strength. If it doesn't, then get closer to their experience. Help and support them. For one thing, this will show you the power of support that you have – and that you have a kind of strength that could be applied to your own life.

How To Be Free From Concern

If you can support others, why not yourself?

Nick Withycombe

Be In Nature More

I've avoided being prescriptive and making statements of 'do this', preferring a lightly entertaining tone with a general outlook on mental health. It's your journey to go on, not another person's dictation to receive.

However, one thing that really does work in living life well is being in nature.

I can say 'be in nature more' with confidence, assuming that a person who already lives and works surrounded by nature is reaping its sanctity and sanity – and therefore won't have been very interested in this topic.

Being in nature is magical, marvellous and medicinal; scientifically proven by many studies. How often are you in nature? How can you increase this in the short term? How can you shift your life to be in nature more in the long term?

Wildlife, greenery, views, clean air and space can elevate your soul to a solacious plain of existence.

SEEK HELP

As said at the start – seek help. If you don't feel 'quite right' then talk to someone. If you feel bad then seek professional help.

The only place I see mentioning 'a social stigma around mental health' is when people are saying there isn't one. Conclusion: there isn't a stigma.

It's not being optimistic or naïve to say that (in British society at least) mental health is not a stigma, not seen as something weird or difficult.

This book is mainly focused on what we can do for ourselves, because that's important. But, simply, talking to others is a must.

Talking to others about your concerns isn't based on an expectation that someone will be able to provide a solution. It also doesn't mean that sharing everything to everyone is always good.

It means talking to either trusted people who are on your side, or health professionals, allows you to vocalise your thoughts. That one simple act can prove to be the mental blessing that people need.

Nick Withycombe

Mantras

Short saying to have ready as supportive, vocal
fall-backs

Best For Me

Many people who experience general concern also worry about how others feel. It's certainly a nice quality – unless you take it too far, causing yourself undue concern.

The mantra 'best for me' sounds odd, but can be useful at times when you are creating un-necessary noise inside your head over how your behaviour – no matter how miniscule – is affecting others.

If you find yourself questioning your actions and mentally fidgeting over if you're being fair to others, it can help to mentally throw your hands up and say 'you know what? Best for me!' and just think of yourself for a change.

Despite talking about ego at the start of this book, it doesn't mean that you cannot simply put yourself first if that's what you deserve. It's not wrong to do the best for yourself.

Nick Withycombe

Correct Decision Made

In this case, I am sure that you are like me; we blame ourselves for making mistakes. This doesn't have to be a bad thing: blaming ourselves doesn't have to be self-harming but can be fun. It's actually a stress release to swear viciously at someone and criticise them – but isn't a very nice thing to do. The good thing about doing this to ourselves is that we won't feel insulted and get mad at ourselves.

However, it's still good to be aware that you aren't wrong. By making a mistake, you aren't bad, you're human.

So, it's good to have the opposite reminder. As most of these mantras, this one sounds very odd and may make me sound like an arrogant moron. I'm OK with that.

I say this to myself when I do something that turns out well. Just as with blaming myself for tiny things, I say this to myself when I have done a tiny thing well. This could be making a correct driving decision that means I either used the least fuel to roll up to the red lights or accelerated just at the right amount to make the green light. It could be something bigger, such as a specific interaction with a specific person.

When it has gone well, I say "correct decision made". It's a way to celebrate

How To Be Free From Concern

small (or big) wins.

It's a way to balance self-blame.

It builds a mental profit/loss of what you've done through the day and it's a positive self-affirmation that you are good at doing things.

Nick Withycombe

No One Cares

The world of well-being tells people that they are important, that they do matter and people do care. This is good. However, it can go the other way.

If you tell people that they are beautiful, when in fact maybe they are not, they will feel pressure to maintain your label of beauty. You can tell someone they are an inspiration but if don't have the experience to deal with the label, they can feel an expectation of maintaining this.

For the concerned amongst us, it can be nice to be out of the spotlight. This isn't saying that we don't like praise and recognition, or we can't be inspiring.

Instead, saying 'no one cares' can be a calming reminder that the pressure and the expectation is living in our heads.

I find it good to remind myself that in many situations, no one cares and it's great that they don't! Only I'm worrying about the thing, no one else is.

It's a short, sharp reminder to stop the mental cyclone and just move on to something else at that moment.

Anxious people can cause themselves anxiety over things that no one else would even notice. It's a tempest of nonsense that exists in your head alone – no one else cares!

Don't Quote Me

This isn't said with anger, it's said with a pleasant smile – dare I say even with a little nonchalance.

This is for when others say "but you said…"

It doesn't mean that you are going back on your word, it means that people can't use what you've said against you. It's giving yourself the freedom and confidence to say something because that was what you thought at the moment – and then new information or simply a new way of thinking has become clear to you.

It's retaining the option of changing your mind without blame. Rather than feeling forced to make a perfect explanation or argue your case – just say that other people shouldn't quote you because that was then and this is now.

Reduce Emotion

This is a difficult question in some senses: when has emotion ever helped you?

When does emotion help us in life? As mentioned previously, emotion is fetishised and we're continually told to care about everything.

It's difficult because simply asking the question can make it sound like advice to not make decisions based on your heart, or to not live a true and authentic life.

But if we're talking about how to be free from concern – and, quite obviously we are because it's the name of the book – then removing emotion can be the single most effective tool in many situations.

Look at it from the perspective of sport: emotion rarely helps. We like to build up the image of the drama of winning or losing – but in the game, the greatest sportspeople remove emotion from their decision-making. While all around them are losing their heads, they stay calm and sometimes take the simplest action available to them.

So, when an interaction with another person or some kind of personal choice is in front of you, saying 'reduce emotion' helps put you in a thought process of removing emotion from the situation rather than adding to it. That, in turn, can lead to

How To Be Free From Concern

simpler consequences and a chain reaction that is more free from concern.

Nick Withycombe

Mental Problems

If I'm having a moment of paranoia, or when I've felt down in the past, I've never thought "hang on, I know what to do right now!" and then taken out my phone for a tearful selfie that I post on social media. But that's just me – it seems to work for others so if that's what they need to do, then have at it.

Instead, I use the mantra and say "mental problems" out loud to myself. It's not self-criticism, it's acceptance; acceptance that a part of my brain is cooking up complete nonsense. I am aware it is complete nonsense so I use the sensible part of my brain to remind myself that it is not real. It is mental problems.

I don't even feel the need to 'fix' these problems any more than I already have done. I accept that they exist – partly because I have the ability to be creative, to be imaginative and to care. These are positive traits, they just also come along with downsides when you start to imagine nonsense.

So when they first pop, I nip them in the bud and reassure myself that the fear is not only fictitious but ridiculous. Saying "mental problems" and literally giving my head a quick shake may seem like a very insane thing to do (try it) but it's actually sane. I promise.

And A Final Word

Finally

The waffle is over and I hope that it has helped.

I'm going to do the classic writer-y thing and take us back to the start: we realise that we may never be totally free from concern, but our dawn of mental awakening is the first light to an ecliptic journey of panoramic sanguinity. Oh crap, more waffle!

We understand that we need to address our minds: awareness.

We may be concerned but that's just how we are: acceptance.

We can feel optimistic by the very desire to feel optimistic: hope.

We are able to identify and dissect our thoughts: knowledge.

We have it within our capability to gain control: empowerment.

I wish you well in your pursuit to be free from concern.

Nick Withycombe

About The Author

Nick is a Dad, a career writer and a life-long worrier. He's procreated, written, lived and worried in several countries and a few continents around the world, sometimes getting married, other times getting divorced and at all times trying to organise the nonsense inside his head.

This book is a result of four decades of mental organisation thus far – it's a token of support, not meant to prevent, cure or solve, but to help, consider and guide us towards greater awareness and better mental health.

More by Nick Withycombe

Find me on the more mature social media platforms out there.

I'll let you know when I get round to writing the next one.

Printed in Great Britain
by Amazon

74563452R00072